Knit
the
Nativity

The Nativity

And it came to pass in those days that a decree went out from Caesar Augustus that all the world should be registered. This census first took place while Quirinius was governing Syria. So all went to be registered, everyone to his own city.

Joseph also went up from Galilee, out of the city of Nazareth, into Judea, to the city of David, which is called Bethlehem, because he was of the house and lineage of David, to be registered with Mary, his betrothed wife, who was with child. So it was, that while they were there, the days were completed for her to be delivered. And she brought forth her firstborn Son, and wrapped Him in swaddling cloths, and laid Him in a manger, because there was no room for them in the inn.

Now there were in the same country shepherds living out in the fields, keeping watch over their flock by night. And behold, an angel of the Lord stood before them, and the glory of the Lord shone around them, and they were greatly afraid. Then the angel said to them, "Do not be afraid, for behold, I bring you good tidings of great joy which will be to all people. For there is born to you this day in the city of David a Saviour, who is Christ the Lord. And this will be the sign to you: You will find a Babe wrapped in swaddling cloths, lying in a manger."

And suddenly there was with the angel a multitude of the heavenly host praising God and saying: "Glory to God in the highest, and on earth peace, goodwill toward men!"

So it was, when the angels had gone away from them into heaven, that the shepherds said to one another, "Let us now go to Bethlehem and see this thing that has come to pass, which the Lord has made known to us." And they came with haste and found Mary and Joseph, and the Babe lying in a manger. Now when they had seen Him, they made widely known the saying which was told them concerning this Child. And all those who heard it marveled at those things which were told them by the shepherds. But Mary kept all these things and pondered them in her heart.

LUKE 2:1–19 (NEW KING JAMES VERSION)

Then Herod, when he had secretly called the wise men, determined from them what time the star appeared. And he sent them to Bethlehem and said, "Go and search carefully for the young Child, and when you have found Him, bring back word to me, that I may come and worship Him also."

When they heard the king, they departed; and behold, the star which they had seen in the East went before them, till it came and stood over where the young Child was. When they saw the star, they rejoiced with exceedingly great joy. And when they had come into the house, they saw the young Child with Mary His mother, and fell down and worshiped Him. And when they had opened their treasures, they presented gifts to Him: gold, frankincense, and myrrh.

MATTHEW 2: 7–11 (NEW KING JAMES VERSION)

Knit
the
Nativity

Jan Messent

Search Press

Acknowledgements

With thanks to Linda Stone for knitting all the pieces.

This edition published in Great Britain 2012

Search Press Limited
Wellwood, North Farm Road,
Tunbridge Wells, Kent TN2 3DR

Text copyright ©Jan Messent 2012

Based on **Knit the Christmas Story** first published by
Search Press Ltd, 1987

Scripture taken from the New King James Version.
Copyright © 1982 by Thomas Nelson, Inc. Used by permission.
All rights reserved.

Photographs by Paul Bricknell at Search Press Photographic Studio

Photographs and design copyright © Search Press Ltd, 2012

The starburst image used on page 2 is reproduced with kind
permission from Christine Gaut

ISBN: 978-1-84448-872-8

The Publishers and author can accept no responsibility for any
consequences arising from the information, advice or instructions
given in this publication.

Suppliers
If you have difficulty in obtaining any of the materials and
equipment mentioned in this book, then please visit the Search
Press website for details of suppliers: www.searchpress.com

Printed in China

Contents

Manger, page 26

Infant, page 28

Shepherd, page 38

Shepherd, page 42

Stable, page 12

Mary, page 16

Joseph, page 22

Ox, page 30

Ass, page 32

Sheep, page 34

Angel, page 46

Shepherd, page 44

Wise Man Casper, page 50
Frankincense, page 60

Wise Man Balthazar, page 54
Myrrh, page 60

Wise Man Melchior, page 58
Gold, p-age 60

Introduction

The most important Christian festival is a time of coming together for families and groups, and what better way could one have than to share the joys of creating the Nativity scene, small enough to be manageable and large enough for all to have a hand in its making, from the older, more experienced knitter, to the youngest beginner.

The patterns are presented in a way which allows for individual interpretation, both of yarns and of stitch patterns, and the simple card figures are easily made from thick 'box card' which can be obtained quite easily. This is where those not so keen on taking part in the knitting activities can be of help. There is even a simple yarn-wrapping activity for young fingers, as the whole of the stable wall is covered in this way.

The knitted garments will provide many hours of enjoyment for those who create them. The materials needed are simple and inexpensive; it should be quite possible to provide all the requirements from home or school.

Knitting and construction

Patterns used

Picot pattern: used to make holes and for lacy effects.
Row 1: *k2tog., y.fwd., rep from * to end of row.
Row 2: p. or k., including the y.fwds. of the previous row.
These 2 rows form the pattern.

Single rib: on an even number of sts., every row is k.1, p.1 to the end.

Double rib: on multiples of four sts., every row is k.2, p.2 to the end.

Moss stitch: on an odd number of sts., every row begins k.1, p.1. and continues like this to the end, thus making the k. and p. sts. move one place on each row.

Double moss stitch: does the same as moss st. with pairs of sts.

Abbreviations

The main stitches used are stocking stitch (i.e. alternate rows of knit and purl), which is abbreviated as s.s., and garter stitch (i.e. every row knitted), which is abbreviated as g.st. Reverse s.s. is the reverse side of stocking stitch, abbreviated as rev.s.s. Other general abbreviations are as follows:

beg.	beginning
dec.	decrease
foll.	following
inc.	increase
k.	knit
k2tog.	knit 2 sts. together
psso.	pass slip st. over
p.	purl
p2tog.	purl 2 sts. together
rem.	remaining
rep.	repeat
R.S.	right side
sl.1	slip 1 st. without knitting it
st(s).	stitch(es)
tog.	together
W.S.	wrong side
y.fwd.	yarn forward
y.r.n.	yarn round needle

Yarn amounts

It is virtually impossible to say how much yarn will be needed for these figures, as so much depends on the varying thickness of D.K. yarns, individual knitting tensions and stitch patterns used, but the largest garment will only need, at most, a 25g ball, and the other parts only very small oddments. The main thing is to acquire a large variety of colours from which to choose, dull ones as well as bright ones, plenty of whites and flesh colours, and browns. The largest part of the project is the stable. The roof/floor is knitted with a heavy rug-type yarn on thicker needles, but the walls, again, are made from oddments wrapped around card strips, and these yarns can be any thickness as long as the colours blend in with each other. This part should be supervised by one person so that an overall unity is achieved in the colours and the 'window landscapes'.

The actual yarns/colours used for each figure are shown separately to help you identify thicknesses and yarn-types, (see Colour Samples, pages 11).

Helpful hints

Curled edges

When knitting small pieces in stocking stitch, such as capes and cloaks, you may find that the edges roll inwards. There are several ways of avoiding this problem; one is to work an edge of garter stitch (about 4–6 sts.) on each side and along the bottom; another way is to work a crochet edge all round, and yet another solution is to pin the piece down flat and press it gently under a damp cloth. Garter stitch, rib patterns and similar dense stitches do not cause this problem.

How to make a cord

Take a piece of yarn at least 152cm (60in) long, fold it in half and knot the two ends together. Loop one end over a door handle, a hook or a friend's finger, and slip a pencil through the loop at the other end. Keep the yarn absolutely straight and taut at all times. Pull away from the hook to tighten the yarn and hold the pencil end of the yarn in the left hand while using your right index finger to rotate the pencil very quickly (like a propeller) round and round in the same direction. This will twist the yarn, keeping it under tension, until it is very tightly twisted indeed. Keep hold of the pencil. Now place your left index finger, (still keeping it under tension), at the centre point of the twisted yarn and move the pencil end to the hook

end, slipping the latter on to the pencil. Now the twisted yarn is folded back upon itself, and as soon as you let go with your left hand, (keep hold of the other ends with your right hand), it will spring up and the two halves will twist together. Slide your left hand down the cord to pull out the kinks and tie the loose end in a knot to prevent it unravelling. You should now have a tight, firm cord.

Box stand to make figures taller

This little stand is a useful method of making some of the standing figures taller so that they can be seen more easily when placed behind others, especially the angel and the three wise men. Cut pieces of card as shown (see Fig 1), and use sticky-tape to hold the four sides in place. Cover the four side edges with a narrow strip of knitting in the same colour as the bottom of the gown, and then stick this in place with glue, making sure that the join is placed at the back. The figure may then be stuck on top and the join will be disguised by the border of the gown.

As an alternative, the size of the figures can be altered by halving, or doubling, the measurements and materials recommended for each one.

Fig 1 *The box stand for the figures*

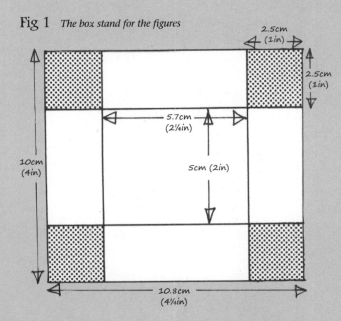

2.5cm (1in)

2.5cm (1in)

5.7cm (2¼in)

10cm (4in)

5cm (2in)

10.8cm (4¼in)

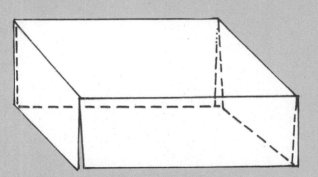

Cut out the shaded squares and score lightly along the remaining lines. Fold as shown above. Stick knitting round edges and leave the top bare.

Materials

* Thick 'box card' – straight, clean, undamaged pieces cut from grocery boxes or bought in a craft shop, and larger pieces for the stable.

* A very sharp craft knife, old scissors, small pliers and wire-cutters.

* Metal ruler and tape-measure.

* Pins, large and small. Stapler – optional but useful.

* Pencils.

* Strong glue such as carpet glue – a large pot.*

* Sticky-tape – strong parcel-tape is useful. Double-sided sticky tape is essential.

* Paper clips and bulldog clips.

* Synthetic wadding for padding – small amounts.

* Needlework scissors and wool (tapestry) needles for sewing.

* A range of knitting needles from size 2.75–6mm (UK 12/US 2–UK 4/US 10) and a medium-sized crochet hook for chains.

* An assortment of double-knitting (D.K.) yarns. Check individual instructions for colours and types, and see separate headings for quantities.

* Useful bits and pieces include small tubular centres from reels of sticky-tape, for head-dresses and gifts, sequins, beads, braids and fancy cords for decoration.

* For the halos and stars, pieces of clear, stiff transparent plastic; either the kind used for small disposable pots from the food counters of grocery stores, or acetate. This should be pliable enough to cut with scissors.

* Pliable wire needed for the shepherds' crooks, (see instructions for specific amounts), or use wooden ones if you prefer.

* Strips of hook and pile fabric fastener to hold the roof in position. This is optional.

*Glue: the use of glue in this project is not a poor substitute for sewing. A good strong glue, carefully applied with a brush, is the best way to attach rigid parts to each other in this kind of project where ease, speed, efficiency and neatness are important. It can be reinforced by staples and sticky-tape if necessary. It is perhaps safer to have an adult in charge of this department.

Colour Samples

Mary

gown   head-
dress   hair   face

Joseph

gown   under-
gown   face   hair

beard

Infant and
manger

gown   face   hair   manger   straw

Animals

donkey   ox   sheep

Kneeling
shepherd

tunic   waistcoat   face   hair   lamb

Shepherd
with jerkin

gown   jerkin   head-
dress   face   beard

Standing
shepherd

gown   head-
dress   face   beard

Angel

gown &
wings   face   hair

Balthazar

cloak   gown   hat   face

Melchior

cloak   tunic   sandals   hair &
face   beard

Caspar

turban   gown and cloak   face

Stable

This must be very sturdy, so thick and rigid card is needed, or even two pieces stapled together for extra strength. Two of these extra strong pieces are needed, each measuring 56 x 36cm (22 x 14in) and these are used for the backing. As well as these, two more pieces to the same measurements are needed but these need not be quite as thick as the first set, as they will be cut into strips and wrapped then stuck down on to the thicker backing. These two inside pieces of slightly thinner card are first cut to make four, (see Fig 2), the smaller pieces being for the windows and the others to be cut into strips.

From the two thinner pieces, cut out 'windows' of 28 x 19cm (11 x 7½in), leaving frames of 4cm (1½in) all round. Cut two spines, (so that the stable will fold away when not in use), measuring 36 x 2.5cm (14 x 1in), one in the very rigid card, and one thinner one to be wrapped. Tape the outer spine in place between the two rigid pieces of card so that it closes like an empty book cover.

The other two pieces, measuring 29 x 36cm (11½ x 14in), now have to be cut into long strips of varying widths ranging from 2–5cm (¾–2in) wide. A craft knife and metal ruler are needed to do this safely and accurately.

Wrapping: down the back side of each strip of card, lay a length of double-sided sticky-tape. Take this to the extreme top and bottom edges, and do not leave gaps. Now with oddments of brown and cream thick yarns, wrap round and round the card neatly so that the strands of yarn lie very closely together, and are pulled fairly tight. If you want to change colour, press the end of the yarn to the sticky back and cut it off, then begin with another in the same way. To lay yarns on top of each other, stick the ends down with ordinary sticky-tape. Take the wrappings from top to bottom of each piece, then lay these in position on the outer piece of card. You may find that the thickness of the yarns makes each strip a little wider, so you will then have to adjust the width of one or two strips to make a perfect fit. Do not stick them down yet. Wrap the inner spine strip too, and stick this in position; a gap must be left at each side of this to allow the walls to close.

Wrap the window frames in the same way, but leave the corners free. These should be coloured

in the same colours as the walls with paint or fibre pen. The two oblongs which were cut out of the window frames now have to be wrapped to resemble the dark night and the eastern sky. Use oddments of yarn to do this in the same way as the strips. Textured yarn can be used too. When all the wrapping is complete, begin by gluing the windows and frames in position, allowing no gaps to be seen between the frame and the window-scene. Then glue the wrapped strips from the window sides towards the centre, so that they lie snugly together. Hold the pieces down with bulldog clips until the glue sets.

For the roof/floor: use thick strong card cut out to the shape, (see Fig 3), then fold the edges down to form a lid and tape these in position. For the knitted cover, a thick chunky yarn is best and you may need as much as 100g as this is certainly the largest knitted piece of the project. Check your knitting from time to time against the card roof/floor and

And she brought forth her firstborn Son, and wrapped Him in swaddling cloths, and laid Him in a manger, because there was no room for them in the inn.
LUKE 2: 7

Fig 2

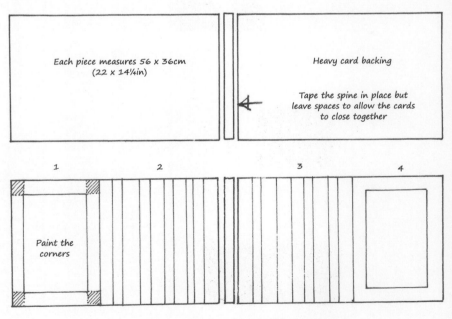

Each piece measures 56 x 36cm (22 x 14¼in)

Heavy card backing

Tape the spine in place but leave spaces to allow the cards to close together

Paint the corners

1   2   3   4

Inner card cut into windows and strips for wrapping

adjust the number of stitches and rows if necessary. The two halves are made separately and joined down the centre, and the front edging is made afterwards and sewn on. If preferred, this section may be used as a floor, on which to place the various figures, (see Fig 4).

With size 6mm (UK 4, US 10) needles, for the left side, (seen from the front), cast on 38 sts.

Knit 2 rows and purl the 3rd row.

Begin the shaping, keeping 5 sts. straight for the centre as folls:

Row 4: k.5, sl.1, k.1, psso., k. to the last 4 sts., k2tog., k.2.
Row 5: p.
Row 6: k.
Row 7: p.

Repeat these 4 rows until only 10 sts. rem. after the last dec. row. Work 3 rows straight.
Next row: k.5, sl.1, k.1, psso., k2tog., k.1. (8sts)
P. one row and cast off.
For the right side, begin with the first 3 rows as before.
Row 4: k.2, sl.1, k.1, psso., k. to the last 7 sts., k2tog., k.5.
Row 5: p.
Row 6: k.
Row 7: p.

Repeat these 4 rows until only 10 sts rem after the last dec row. Work 3 rows straight.

Next row: k.1, sl.1, k.1, psso., k2tog., k.5.

P. one row and cast off.

Fig 3

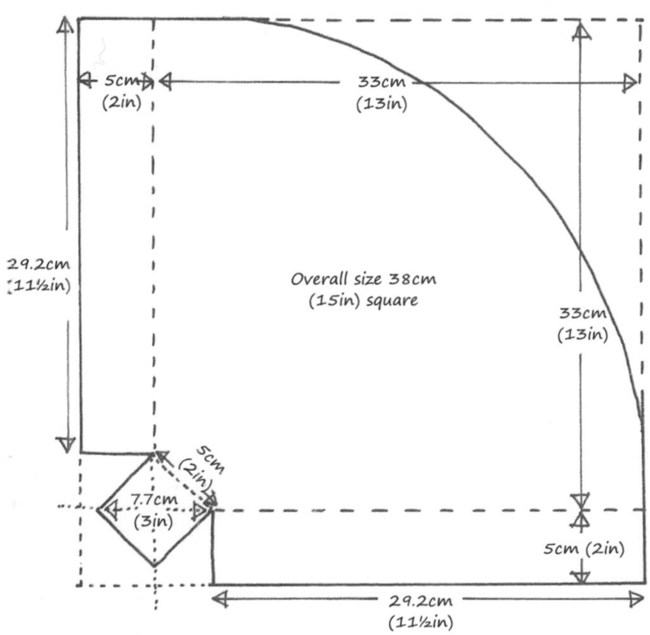

Roof/floor

5cm (2in)
33cm (13in)
29.2cm (11½in)
Overall size 38cm (15in) square
33cm (13in)
5cm (2in)
7.7cm (3in)
5cm (2in)
29.2cm (11½in)

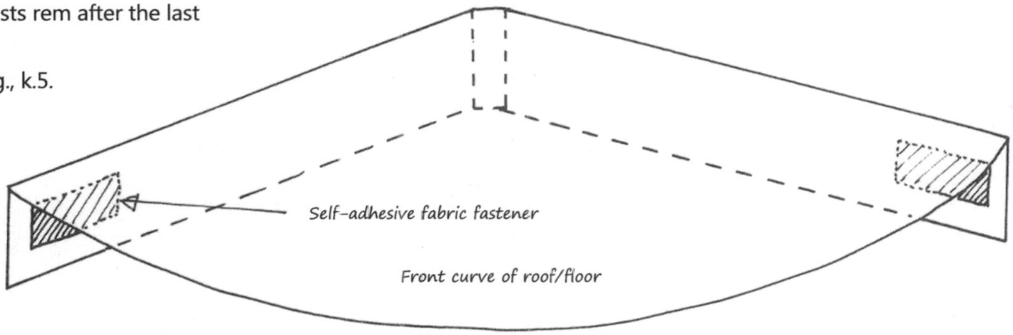

Fig 4

Self-adhesive fabric fastener

Front curve of roof/floor

With the two widest borders and R.S.s tog., pin the two roof/floor sections tog. and sew up the centre seam. Fit the card roof shape on to the corner of a table and place glue along the curved front edge, then stick the front edge of the knitted piece to this, allowing the first row to hang over the edge so that the border can be stitched on. Now glue along each side and a little way down from the top edge. Press the sides of knitting on to these edges and then glue the short back edge. The gluing may be reinforced by staples if necessary.

Make a narrow decorative border for the top edge, using the same yarn and needles, by casting on 5 sts.

Knit 4 rows. Cast off 3 sts. at the beg. of the next row. Knit 3 rows on the rem. 2 sts. Cast on 3 sts.

Repeat these rows until the border is long enough to stretch from one corner to the other, then cast off. Stitch it to the overhanging edge of the roof/floor sections, and allow it to hang downwards as shown, with the extreme end 'flap' lying on top of the wall at each side.

To keep the stable roof in place, use self-adhesive hook and pile fabric strips at the extreme edge of the back flap, and also in the adjoining place on the back wall of the stable. The pieces will not show from outside, (see Fig 4).

13

The stars

To make the large star in the east, (see right), work the centre part in exactly the same way as the halos, (see page 21). Use fine, white/silver glittery yarn and follow the same instructions. The outer ring of points requires the same kind of transparent backing as for the halos, but measures about 11 cm (4¼in) in diameter. Punch holes about 1cm (⅜in) apart but make these on the edge so that notches are made, rather than complete holes, (see Fig 5 opposite).

Using the chosen yarn, glue the beginning of this to the centre of the circle with sticky-tape, then wind across the circle from notch to notch, making two complete circuits. It helps to have an even number of holes, but this is not vitally important. Cut the thread and stick the end to the centre. Now glue the knitted centre-piece (see page 21) on top of this wrapped piece and then glue both of these to the background landscape.

The smaller stars are made in the same way as described above without the extra knitted centre-piece and using smaller circles. These can be drawn round small coins.

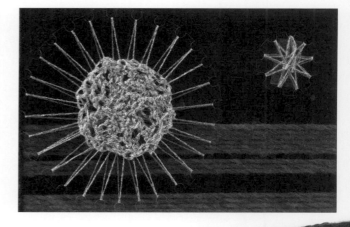

Behold, the star which they had seen in the East went before them, till it came and stood over where the young Child was. When they saw the star, they rejoiced with exceedingly great joy.

MATTHEW 2:9–10

14

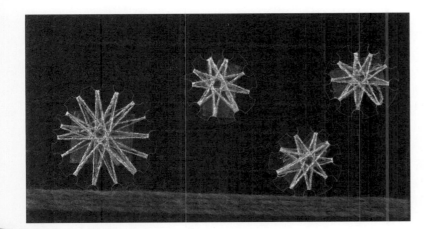

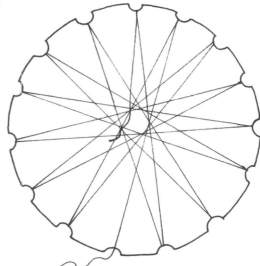

Fig 5
Star

Yarn ready to go round second time
(direction not important)

Oddments of contrasting yarn are wrapped round strips of card and glued to a rigid card backing to create the stable. The knitted stars are then added to the background landscape.

15

Mary and Joseph

Fig 6

Mary, the seated figure

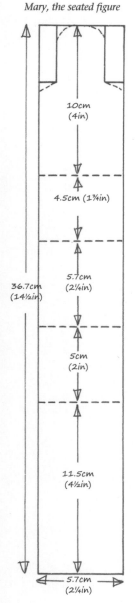

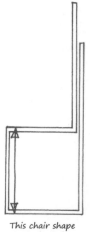

This chair shape is the basis for the sitting figure and may be glued or stapled in position, with tape wrapped round the back.

10cm
(4in)

4.5cm (1¾in)

5.7cm
(2¼in)

5cm
(2in)

11.5cm
(4½in)

36.7cm
(14½in)

5.7cm
(2¼in)

Mary

Make the card base for Mary (see Fig 6). This figure sits on a boulder, (see Fig 7a, page 18) made from a long rectangle of knitting fixed around the back and sides of the base. Her skirt and bodice are made all-in-one piece and the arms and hands are made separately then sewn to the shoulders.

Begin by making the face from pink D.K. yarn on size 3mm (UK 11, US 3) needles. Cast on 12 sts. and work 18 rows in s.s. Cast off and attach to the head over the padding (see Fig 9, page 19). This is the face pattern for all the adult figures.

The boulder on which Mary sits is made of grey D.K. yarn. Only a small amount of this is needed. Using 3.75mm (UK 9, US 5) needles, cast on 40 sts. and work in double moss st., (or garter st.), until the piece measures 19 x 6.5cm (7½ x 2½in). Cast off and glue to the back and the two sides, allowing it to overlap slightly on to the front edge.

The dress will require about 20g of pale blue D.K. yarn and size 3.75mm (UK 9, US 5) needles. Cast on 40 sts., knit 4 rows and purl the 5th. Continue in s.s. for 30 rows, noting that this piece should measure 11.5cm (4¼in) deep at this stage. Now reduce the 40 sts. to half this number by k.2tog. all along the row. This point is the waist.

Next row: p.20 sts.

At the beg. of the next 2 rows, cast on 6 sts. and work in s.s. until 16 rows altogether have been worked on these 32 sts., ending with a p. row. This section should measure 5cm (2in) from the waist. Now reduce the sts. for the shoulders and neck as folls:

Next row: k.4, (k2tog.) 12 times, k.4.
Next row: k. Cast off.

To attach the dress to the card figure, fit the neck and pin in position, neatly back-stitch this to the knitting underneath, then continue down the back to join the two edges together from neck to waist. Cut a small square piece of padding and insert this between the card and the knitting at the front to slightly pad the figure. Sew the lower edge of the back section to the knitted boulder, leaving the side edges of the skirt free at this stage.

Then the angel said to her, "Do not be afraid, Mary, for you have found favour with God. And behold, you will conceive in your womb and bring forth a Son, and shall call His name Jesus."

LUKE 1:30–31

Take the side edges of the skirt and pin them to the front corners of the boulder, stitch in place, then turn in the corners of the skirt and stitch lightly to make the front edge and side seams into a continuous curve, (see Fig 7a).

For the sleeves, use the same yarn and size 3mm (UK 11, US 3) needles. Leave a length of yarn for sewing and cast on 4 sts. Work 2 rows in s.s., then inc. 1 st. at each end of every k. row until there are 16 sts.

Beginning with a p. row, continue straight in s.s. for 12 more rows.

Next row: (W.S. facing) k.
Next row: (k2tog., k.5) twice, k2tog.
Next row: k.
Next row: (k2tog., k.2) twice, k2tog., k.3 (10sts.)
Next row: k.

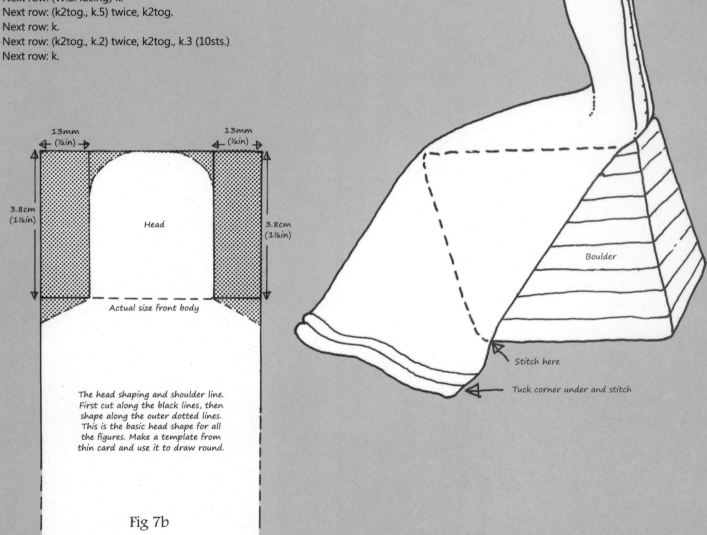

Fig 7a

Boulder

Stitch here

Tuck corner under and stitch

13mm (½in)

13mm (½in)

3.8cm (1½in)

3.8cm (1½in)

Head

Actual size front body

The head shaping and shoulder line. First cut along the black lines, then shape along the outer dotted lines. This is the basic head shape for all the figures. Make a template from thin card and use it to draw round.

Fig 7b

18

Change to pink yarn (R.S. facing) and work 6 rows in s.s. Run thread through stitches and pull up. With R.S.s tog. sew the hand side seams, then white sleeve seam as far as shaping. Leave the rest of the sleeve open. Make another one in the same way. No padding is needed for the hands or the arms. Attach the 4 cast-on sts. to the top of the shoulder next to the neckband, and sew round the sleeve opening to the bodice.

The head-dress is a large triangular piece of knitting in s.s. You will need a medium sized ball of pure white D.K. yarn and size 3.75mm (UK 9, US 5) needles.

Cast on 60 sts. and work 4 rows of s.s., then dec. at each end of every k. row until 2 sts. rem. Cast off. To neaten the long edge, (which goes over the top of the head), you may wish to work one row of double crochet. This is necessary to stop the front curling. Make the hair from a strip of brown knitting and sew this in place, (only the top of the head shows), and then embroider the face. Wrap the white head-dress around the figure as shown and stitch this in place, (see Fig 8).

Attach halo to back of head-dress, (see page 21 for instructions).

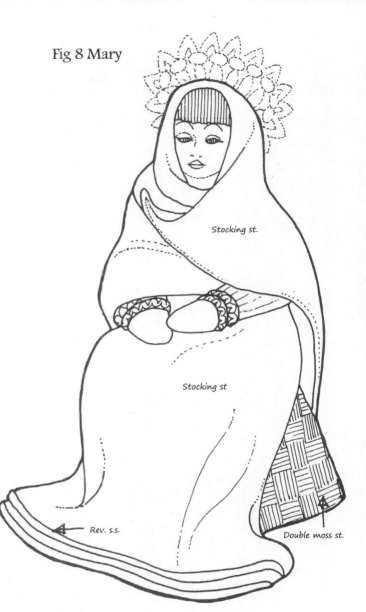

Fig 8 Mary

Stocking st.

Stocking st

Rev. s.s.

Double moss st.

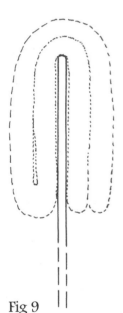

Fig 9

The head and face, actual size. This is the pattern for all the adult figures.

Card seen from the side with padding in place on the head. Cut a strip of padding 6mm (¼in) thick and 20.3cm (8in) long x 3.2cm (1¼in) wide. Fold this in half and place over the head as shown. Staple or glue this in place at the neck. This padding gives extra height to the figure.

Padding

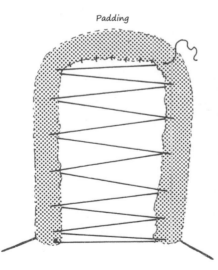

Face covering seen from the back. Each face is covered by a small piece of flesh-coloured knitting which is sewn over the padding. This is then covered by hair and/or beard. Use any flesh-coloured yarn in D.K. thickness of 3mm needles. Cast on 12 sts. and work 18 rows of s.s. Cast off. Pin this piece in place on the head, taking the side edges well round to the back. Pull the lower edge down on to the neck. Now stitch this on to the padding at the top and lace the two side edges across the back as shown.

19

Joseph also went up from Galilee, out of the city of Nazareth, into Judea, to the city of David, which is called Bethlehem, because he was of the house and lineage of David, to be registered with Mary, his betrothed wife, who was with child. So it was, that while they were there, the days were completed for her to be delivered.

LUKE 2: 4–5

The halos

The instructions for these are rather general, as the exact size, pattern and effect will depend on the various factors involved such as yarn type and number of stitches needed. The idea is extremely simple and does not require circular knitting or complicated stitches. Try a 'sample' first and then you will be able to judge the best size and yarn.

The base is a circular piece of pliable transparent plastic, (you can cut this from the bottom of disposable food containers, or use thick acetate), which has had holes punched in it round the edge. You can do this with an ordinary paper punch. The disc should be about the size shown in the diagrams, (see right), but this is not critical, and the holes should be spaced evenly.

Fine glittery yarn is best, gold for the most striking effect, and needles varying from sizes 3 to 6mm (UK 11/US 3–UK 4/US 10)You will need the same number of stitches as there are holes, or double the number so that you can lace through every alternate stitch if you prefer. It is the lacing thread which makes the points. To cast on, an easy loose method is used: instead of making each new stitch from between the last two, insert the needle into the previous stitch and make it from this one to achieve a loopy edge.

Now make a narrow strip of knitting and begin by knitting one row, then work 2 or 4 rows of picot pattern, (see page 8). Make the 2nd row of the pattern k. instead of p. Remember that the last row of the knitting is the centre of the circle, (gathered up), and the cast on edge goes to the outer edge, so very few rows are needed. On the last row, k2tog. across all sts. to make half as many, then slip the last row on to a long length of the same yarn. Gather the centre up and sew the two short sides to form a circle.

Place the circular piece of knitting in the centre of the plastic disc and use the length of yarn to lace through the holes, over the edge and through the stitches. Do this all the way round to make the points, then fasten off securely. You can use either side of the knitting, whichever is most pleasing.

The halos are stuck to the back of the heads with glue, and the transparent backing allows the lacy effect to be seen from both sides.

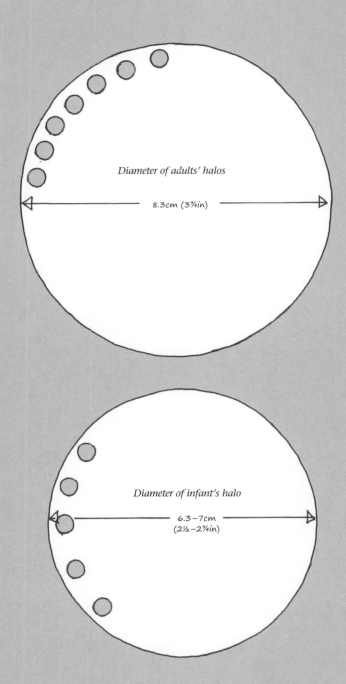

Diameter of adults' halos

8.3cm (3¼in)

Diameter of infant's halo

6.3–7cm
(2½–2¾in)

21

Joseph

Joseph is the next figure in our story. Make the card base for a standing figure, (see Figs 11 and 12).

Begin by making the face as for Mary, but from tan D.K. yarn, and embroider features.

For the hair, use a small amount of dark brown D.K. yarn and 3mm (UK 11, US 3) needles, (see Fig 10 below). I have used dark brown eyelash yarn for the beard. If you use this, you might need to trim the beard a little to tidy it up!

Cast on 12 sts. and work in g.st. for 30 rows.
Next row: cast off 7 sts. and k. to end of row.

Work on the rem. 5 sts. for 12 more rows, then cast off. Gather the top of the hair piece and draw up to fit the top of the head. Fit this in place and glue to the head. Sew the edge of the beard to the other side of the face and stick with a tiny dab of glue, pulling it down into a slight curve. Make a gold cord and fasten this around the head, (see Fig 8, page 24).

Joseph's cream undergown is simply a rectangle of knitting stuck on to the front section of the card base, with the cast off edge at the top. A small amount of cream/white D.K. yarn is needed, and size 3.75mm (UK 9, US 5) needles, or size 4mm (UK 8, US 6). Cast on 12 sts. and k. 2 rows, then continue in s.s. as far as the neck – about 19cm (7½in). Stick this in place with glue and make a cord to tie round the front card section only.

Joseph's brown gown is knitted lengthwise, (i.e. from one side edge to the other side), in s.s. with rev. s.s. ridges. It wraps completely round the card body and slightly overlaps the undergown at each side. Use 3.75mm (UK 9, US 5) needles and brown D.K. yarn. Cast on 40 sts. and k. 2 rows, p. the next row, then k. 3 rows.

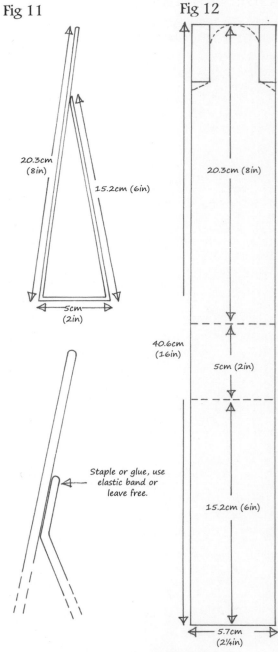

Fig 11

Fig 12

20.3cm (8in)

15.2cm (6in)

5cm (2in)

40.6cm (16in)

20.3cm (8in)

5cm (2in)

15.2cm (6in)

5.7cm (2¼in)

Staple or glue, use elastic band or leave free.

The card base for standing figures

Shape head and shoulders as shown and score lightly along the dotted lines to fold into the shape seen in the top diagram.

Fig 10

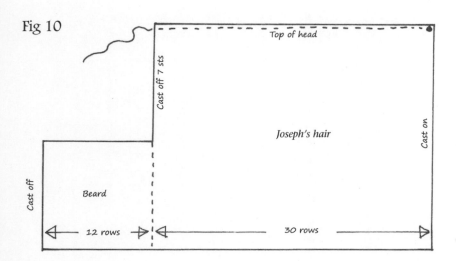

Top of head

Cast off 7 sts

Joseph's hair

Cast on

Cast off

Beard

12 rows

30 rows

Next row: k.4, p. to the end.

Knit the next 3 rows. Repeat the last 4 rows until the piece measures 17.5cm (7in) ending with a p. row.

Next row: (R.S.) p.
Next row: (W.S.) k. Cast off.

Fasten off all ends and gather the neckline with double yarn and draw up to fit the neck to make a collar as shown, (see Fig 9, page 19).

The brown outer sleeve is made separately from the white sleeve and hands, and the two pieces are then sewn together. For the brown sleeve, cast on 16 sts. and k. 2 rows. Continue in s.s. for 13 more rows, beginning with a p. row.

Next row: (k2tog., k.5) twice, then k2tog.
Next row: p.
Next row: k2tog., k.2, k2tog., k.1., k2tog., k.2, k2tog. (9 sts.)
Next row: p.
Next row: (k2tog.) twice, k.1, (k2tog.) twice, (5 sts.)
Next row: p.5, then cast off.

...behold, an angel of the Lord appeared to him in a dream, saying, "Joseph, son of David, do not be afraid to take to you Mary your wife, for that which is conceived in her is of the Holy Spirit. And she will bring forth a Son, and you shall call His name Jesus, for He will save His people from their sins."

MATTHEW 1:20–21

Sew up the side edges from the cast-on edge towards the top, leaving half the side open to attach to the body. For the cream undersleeves and hands, begin with the same yarn and needles as before, cast on 10 sts. and work 7 rows in s.s. Knit the 8th row.

Change to size 3mm (UK 11, US 3) needles and tan yarn (as for face). Work 4 rows of s.s., and thread the last row on to a length of yarn and gather up to form the hand. Sew the hand up the two side edges, then the cream sleeve. Place a tiny amount of padding into the hand, leaving the rest of the sleeve empty. Insert the brown sleeve top into the outer (brown) sleeve end, and sew round the edge.

Attach each sleeve/hand to the body at the shoulder of the gown, with the top (cast-off) edge on the gathered neckline. Sew all round the sleeve opening, attaching it to the garment so that it lies flat and straight. Make a cord of the same yarn and thread this through the neck gathers. Fit the gown on to the figure and arrange the neckline to leave a gap of about 2.5cm (1in) across the front. Tie the cord into a bow. Bring the two front edges of the gown on to the cream undergown, overlapping slightly, then stitch in place as far as the collar.

Attach halo to back of head, (see page 21 for instructions).

Fig 8 Joseph

Opposite
Joseph with the ass (see pages 32–33).

Rev. s.s. ribs

G. st. border

Manger

This is the centrepiece of the Christmas story and it must be large enough to accommodate the figure and robe of the Infant, (see page 28).

Yarns: light brown D.K. yarn and yellow yarn.

Cut three pieces of card, one 12.7cm (5in) square, and two 7.6 x 5cm (3 x 2in), score and fold, (see Fig 13). These pieces are not glued together but are first covered by knitted rectangles, then sewn.

Use pale brown D.K. yarn and size 4mm (UK 8, US 6) needles. Cast on 31 sts. and work the following pattern:

Row 1: * k.3, p.1, rep. from * to the last 3 sts., k. 3.
Row 2: * p.3, k.1, rep. from * to the last 3 sts., p. 3.

Repeat these two rows until there are 22 rows from the beginning. Change to yellow yarn and work in rev. s.s. as follows: k. the first 2 rows then p. the next one and continue in rev. s.s. until 28 rows of the yellow have been worked. If the piece looks as though it might be too wide with the new yarn, change to a finer needle size. This piece should measure 9cm (3½in). With the R.S. facing, change back to brown yarn and pattern as before for 22 rows. Cast off in pattern.

With R.S.s tog., fold the 2 short edges towards the centre and pin in position, (see Fig 13). Sew up along the folded sides leaving an opening in the centre (i.e. the cast on and cast off edges), where the card can be slipped inside. Fit the card corners into position neatly, then sew up the opening so that the seam lies along the bottom of the manger.

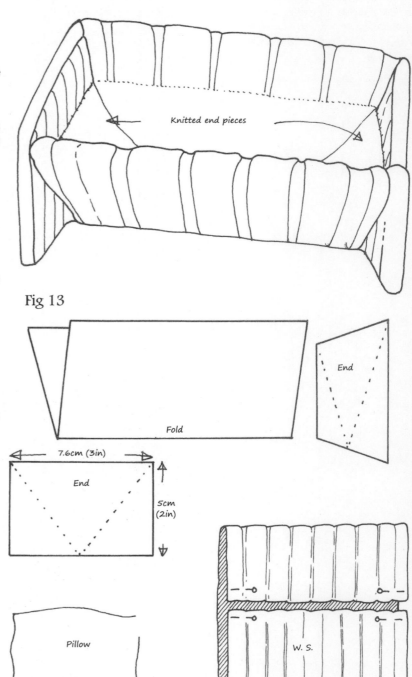

Knitted end pieces

Fig 13

Fold

End

7.6cm (3in)

End

5cm (2in)

12.7cm (5in)

12.7cm (5in)

Score along here

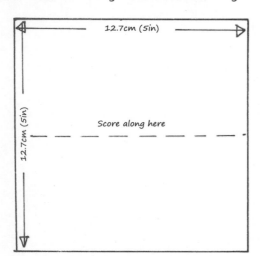

Pillow

W. S.

For the two end panels, cast on 15 sts. and work in the same 3 x 1 rib for 14 rows. Work one p. row, then 14 more rows in pattern. Cast off on a W.S. row. Fold in half, R.S.s tog., and sew up the side edges.

Slip the card inside the pocket and sew up the bottom edge. Make the other side in the same way.

To make the yellow end pieces for the inside of the manger, cast on 10 sts. and knit 6 rows. Now dec. 1 st. at each end of the 7th, 9th, 11th and 13th rows, then cast off. Make another in the same way. Pin each piece on to the loose side panels, with the cast on edges level with the same colour on the main sections, (i.e. about 1cm/³⁄₈in) down from the top edge). Sew this along the top but not down the sides. Take the points and pull them into the manger, then sew these down while the sides are still lying flat. Now fix the two side panels to the main section by sewing them together at each corner and at the underneath points.

To finish off, it may be necessary to tighten the knitted cover by taking stitches through the outer and inner covers and through the card at the bottom of the manger. Fasten off securely.

To make the pillow, use yellow yarn and size 3.75mm (UK 9, US 5) needles. Cast on 10 sts. and work 20 rows in rev.s.s. Cast off.

Fold across, place padding inside and sew up.

You may wish to pad the bottom of the manger with a small amount of chopped yellow yarn for straw.

Infant

The baby Jesus is the most important figure in our story.

Yarns: white D.K. sparkling yarn and pale flesh colour for the face.
A tiny amount of dark yarn for the hair.

The gown: this is knitted in an easy scallop st., but may be made plain
if preferred. Using white sparkling yarn on size 3.75mm (UK 9, US 5)
needles, cast on 29 sts. and k. 3 rows. Then work in pattern as folls.:

Row 1: (y.r.n., k.3, sl.1, k2tog., psso., k.3, y.fwd., k.1) twice, then y.fwd, k.3,
sl.1, k2tog., psso., k.3.
Row 2: y.r.n., and p. to end of the row.
Row 3: as row 1.
Row 4: y.r.n., and k. to end of the row.

Repeat these 4 rows until work measures about 8cm (3¼in) of
pattern, then finish with 2 k. rows.

Fig 14

Now k2tog. across 28 sts., last stitch k.1 to make 15 sts., then k. 1 more row. Change to size 3mm (UK 11, US 3) needles and pale flesh-coloured yarn. Work 7 rows in s.s., then p2tog. across all sts. to make 8. Draw these 8 sts. on to a length of yarn to form the top of the head.

With R.S.s tog., sew down the back and pad the shape very lightly towards the head end. Run a small gathering st. around the neck, gently draw up and secure. Catch the lower edges of the gown together with a small stitch if it is scalloped as in the pattern, but if it is a straight edge, it will have to be sewn right across.

Using dark yarn, thread up a sewing needle and take sts. round the head for the hair, with shorter sts. over the forehead. Embroider the eyes and mouth with finer yarn.

Attach halo to back of head, (see page 21).

Animals

The ox

Cut the base shapes from thick, strong card (see Fig 15 opposite) and tape the two body pieces across the back. Knitting instructions are for use with a chunky tweedy yarn, but if you are using something different, you can check your measurements against the card shape as you go along. You will probably need almost a 50g ball of yarn for this, and some tiny amounts of white, pink and ivory yarn for the details.

Use size 4mm (UK 8, US 9) needles and begin with the four legs, all the same. Cast on 10 sts. and work in s.s. for 10 rows, then cast off. Make three more in the same way, sew up the bottom and side edges and slip these shapes on to the legs.

To make the body, cast on 34 sts. and work 2 rows in single rib. Dec 1 st. at both ends of the next row, then p. one row. (32 sts.). Work 28 more rows of s.s., then inc. 1 st. at each end of the next row, then p. one more row, (34 sts.). Now work 3 rows in single rib, then cast off in rib. Fold the fabric in half and sew the two side edges together (R.S.s tog.), turn to the R.S. and slip this shape on to the card body. Sew the tops of the knitted legs to the ribbed edge, and glue the rest of the lower ribbed edge in place.

To make the head, cast on 14 sts. and work in s.s. for 8 rows. Now dec. 1 st. at each end of the next and every foll k. row until there are only 6 sts. left. Cast off p.wise. This piece should now be folded in half lengthways and used to enclose the head of double-card, the cast on edge being the top of the neck to the poll, and the cast off edge being the nose. Sew these two parts, and the dec. edge, but leave the neck open to be sewn to the body, each side separately. Do not attach the head at this point.

Make the pink nose and white face separately. With pink D.K. yarn and size 3mm (UK 11, US 3) needles, cast on 6 sts. and k. 5 rows. Change to white D.K. yarn and work in s.s. for 10 rows, beginning with a k. row. Now inc. 1 st. at end of the next and foll. k. row until there are 10 sts. P. one more row. Now dec. 1 st. at the end of the next 3 k. rows, then cast off p. wise. Sew this piece to the front face, keeping the pink nose well up on the flat part and allowing the top (white) edge to carry on over the top of the head.

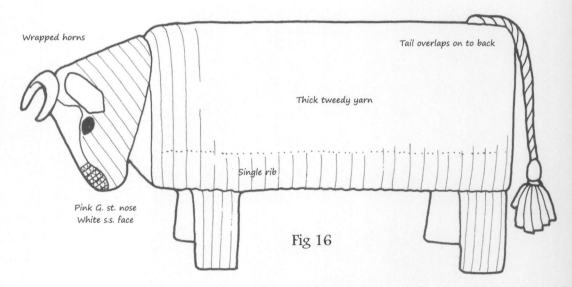

Wrapped horns

Tail overlaps on to back

Thick tweedy yarn

Single rib

Pink G. st. nose
White s.s. face

Fig 16

Make the ears, with the chunky yarn, and size 3.75mm needles, cast on 4 sts. and work 6 rows in s.s.

Next row: (k2tog.) twice and cast off.

Make another to match, and sew to the head as shown. Embroider the eyes in dark yarn. Now pin the head to the body and sew round the neck opening, then lower the chin on to the chest and stitch it in this position to keep the head lowered. Make the tail from a cord, crochet chain or narrow plait with a tassel on the end.

The horns, (optional) are made from two pipe-cleaners, or a 15cm (6in) length of wire bent double, to make four 7.5cm (3in) lengths. This is then wrapped very tightly with ivory yarn, piling up towards the centre. Bend this into shape as shown and stitch, with the same yarn, over and over into the forehead, (see Fig 16).

Fig 15 (actual size)

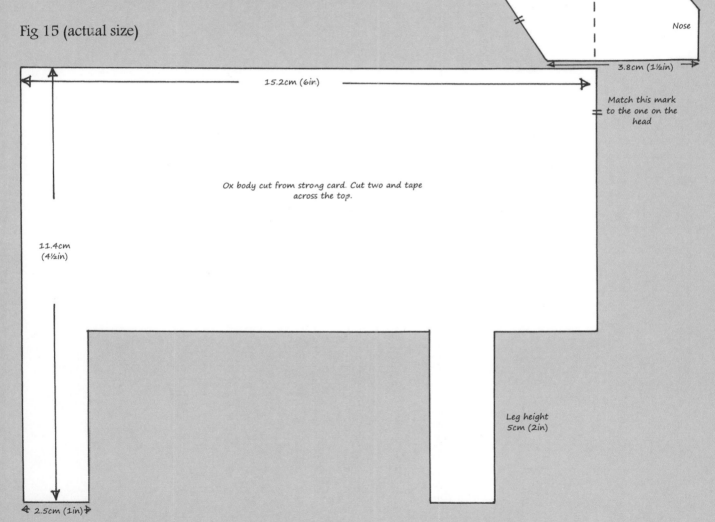

Height
4.6cm
(1¾in)

Head (cut two)

Score very
lightly

Nose

3.8cm (1½in)

15.2cm (6in)

Match this mark
to the one on the
head

Ox body cut from strong card. Cut two and tape
across the top.

11.4cm
(4½in)

Leg height
5cm (2in)

2.5cm (1in)

The ass

This is made from a pale brown D.K. yarn , but any other donkey-colour will do just as well. Cut the card body shape, (see Fig 17 opposite), score along the back very lightly and fold across to make two sides.

Use size 3.75mm (UK 9, US 5) needles and begin with the legs, (all the same). Cast on 8 sts. and work 14 rows in s.s., then cast off. Fold in half lengthways (R.S.s tog.) and sew up the foot end and side edges, then slip this on to the card leg. Make three more.

To make the body, cast on 32 sts. and work in single rib for 33 rows. Cast off. With R.S.s tog., fold across and sew up the side edges, turn to the R.S. then slip this shape on to the card body. Sew the tops of the legs to the body and glue the in-between parts to the card.

To make the head, cast on 12 sts. and work 14 rows in s.s. Change to moss st. and work 16 more rows, then cast off.

With R.S.s tog., fold across the line between the two sets of sts. and sew up one side. Turn to the R.S. and squeeze it diagonally to form a triangle. Fit the card pieces into this with the blunt nose end at the s.s. side, and the neck at the moss st. side. Sew up the s.s. side only from the nose to the centre line.

Make the ears by casting on 6 sts. and working 8 rows in s.s. Dec. 1 st. at each end of the next and the foll. k. row, then cast off. Darn the cast off end in and sew the ears to the head, angled slightly forward as shown. Embroider a large, dark eye on each side of the head.

Make a thick plait from 12 strands of white D.K. yarn and tie this at one end to leave a bunch of strands for the forelock. Sew this to the top of the head between the ears. Now attach the head and neck to the body with stitches on both sides of the neck, matching the central line with the front edge of the body. Complete the sewing of the mane to the neck, taking the end just on to the body. Make a tail from a white crochet chain, a twisted cord or a fine plait and leave a long tassel at the end. Sew this on to the rump, (see Fig 18).

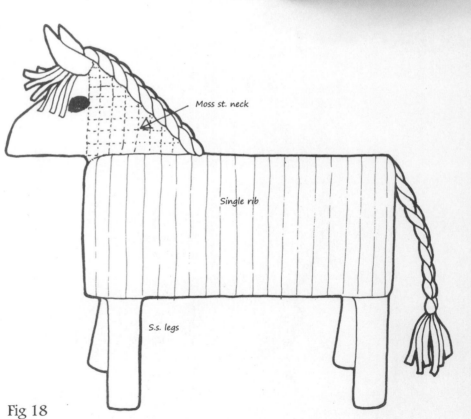

Moss st. neck

Single rib

S.s. legs

Fig 18

Fig 17 (actual size)

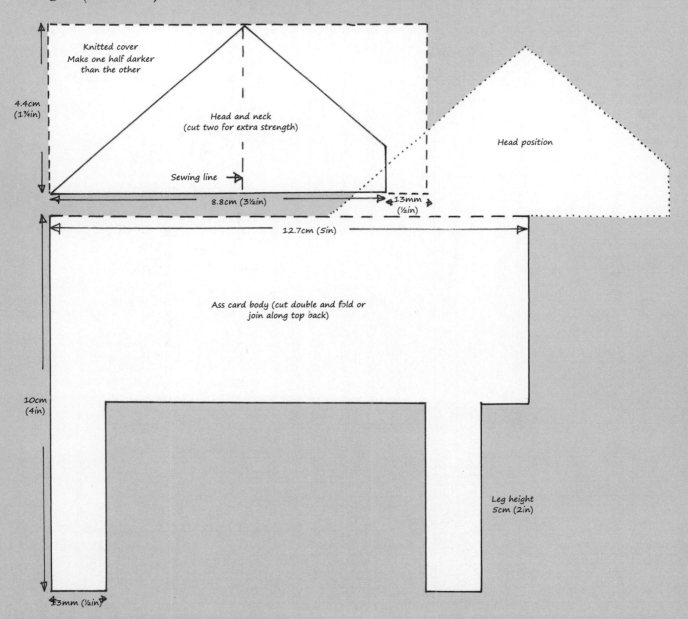

Knitted cover
Make one half darker
than the other

4.4cm
(1¾in)

Head and neck
(cut two for extra strength)

Head position

Sewing line

8.8cm (3½in)

13mm
(½in)

12.7cm (5in)

Ass card body (cut double and fold or
join along top back)

10cm
(4in)

Leg height
5cm (2in)

13mm (½in)

33

The sheep

Cut card pieces, (see Fig 19), and fold the body piece across the centre to form the tent-shaped body. You may need to score lightly across the line first. Cut two head pieces and use them together for extra strength. No legs are needed for this long-wool breed!

· The body cover is simply a rectangle of knitting the same shape and size as the card. The exact number of stitches and rows will depend on the yarn you choose, and the stitch pattern too, but sheep are found in a variety of natural colours ranging from black to white, some both. You will only need very small amounts of yarn; a 25g ball will make several sheep. If you wish to make a short-wool breed, make the knitted body-cover shorter and draw, (or paint), legs on the card to show below the 'wool'. To make a lying-down sheep, cut the card a little shorter (i.e. not so deep) and make the knitted cover to match. Try putting the head on at different angles for variety. Look at photographs to give you ideas.

The sheep body pattern is worked in moss stitch rib, as foll.:

Row 1: * k.3, p.1, rep. from * to the end of the row.
Row 2: * k.2, p.1, k.1, rep from * to the end of the row.

These 2 rows form the pattern. Repeat them for the required length.

Use either double 4 ply (US sportweight) or heavy D.K. yarn on size 3.75mm (UK 9, US 5)needles and cast on 24 sts. Work in pattern for 13.5cm (5¼in). Cast off and fold across the centre, R.S.s tog. Sew the two side edges tog., turn to the R.S., and slip this on to the card body. Glue the lower edges in place.

To make the head, cast on 10 sts. and work in s.s. for 10 rows. This is the neck. Now k. the p. rows, and p. the k. rows for the face, using either the same yarn or a paler or darker one. Work 10 rows then cast off. Fold this piece diagonally as shown by the dotted lines in the diagram, (see Fig 19 opposite), and sew up one side edge. The smooth side of the knitting is for the face with the blunt nose, and the rough side of the knitting is for the neck. Tuck the card inside and fold in the nose point. Sew all round and then embroider the eyes. Make two ears by casting on 4 sts. and then cast them off again without working any rows of knitting. Sew these on each side, then attach the head to the body in any of the positions shown in the illustrations, (see Fig 20 opposite).

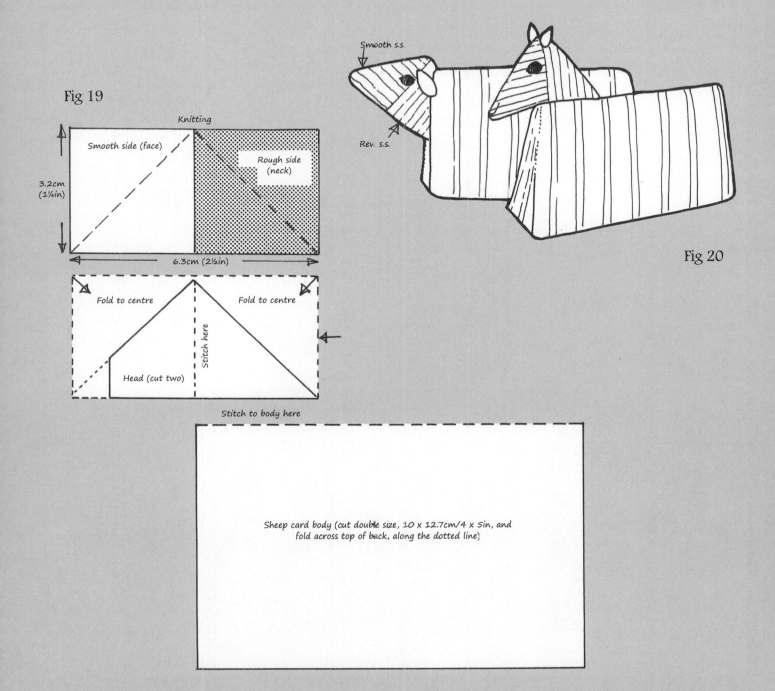

Fig 19

Knitting

Smooth side (face)

Rough side (neck)

3.2cm (1¼in)

6.3cm (2½in)

Fold to centre

Fold to centre

Stitch here

Head (cut two)

Stitch to body here

Sheep card body (cut double size, 10 x 12.7cm/4 x 5in, and fold across top of back, along the dotted line)

Smooth s.s.

Rev. s.s.

Fig 20

Shepherds

Kneeling shepherd

This figure wears a brown textured tunic with long sleeves and a short waistco (vest) over this. He holds a lamb in his arms, and has feet showing underneath lower edge of his tunic. On his head he wears a single band like Joseph's. Mal face, hair and head band in the same way as Joseph's (though I have used or yarn rather than eyelash yarn for this shepherd's beard).

For the tunic, a chunky Aran-type yarn was used, so measurements have be given so that you can keep a check on the size as your work develops. The tu should measure 22cm (8¾in) across the lower edge. With size 4mm (UK 8, US needles, cast on 40 sts. and work 8 rows in s.s., i.e. 4cm (1½in).

Next row (dec. row): (k2tog., k.2) 10 times, (30 sts.).

Work on these 30 sts. for 9 more rows in s.s., i.e. 7cm (2¾in) from the cast on

Next row (dec. row): (k2tog., k.3) 6 times, (24 sts.).

This should be wide enough to go easily round the top of the figure, i.e. 15c (6 in) wide. Work straight, without shaping, to the n

Last row: k2tog. across all sts., then cast off.

Pin the piece in position round the figure and sew up the back seam, then sew the neckline to the lowe edge of the hair. Embroider the eyes and fix the hea band in position.

To make the sleeves, use the same yarn and needles and cast on 4 sts. Work 2 rows in s.s. Inc 1 st. at each end of every k. row until there are 14 sts. noting that the piece should be 7.5cm (3in) wide at this point.

Continue straight until the piece measures 7cm (2¾in) from the cast on edge, ending with a knit row. Knit the next row then change to size 3mm (UK 11, US 3) needles and the same yarn as for the face. Begin with a k. row and work 4 rows in s.s.

Next row (dec. row): (k2tog., k.4) twice, k2tog., (11 sts.).

Work on these 11 sts. for 3 more rows, then gather them on to a thread and draw up to form the end of the hand. Sew up the side edges as far as the shaping, pin the sleeve/hand to the shoulder of the tunic and stitch in position as with the other figures.

To make the feet, first make the card base (see Fig 22) then make a single piece to cover this as folls: with a small amount of dark yarn to represent the soles of the sandals, and size 3mm (UK 11, US 3) needles, cast on 14 sts. Work 6 rows in rev.s.s., then change to flesh colour. Do not cut the first yarn. Purl one row and knit the next. Cut off the flesh-coloured yarn and pick up the first yarn and purl the next 2 rows. Work 6 more rows in rev.s.s. then cast off, making a square of 4.5cm (1¾in). The pale line divides the two feet. Fold this piece in half and sew up the two sides.

Slip the card foot shape inside, and glue this piece in position with the flat base underneath the figure and the short edge against the lower back as shown in Fig 21 opposite. The edge of the tunic can now be glued in position all round the base, slightly overlapping the feet.

> Now there were in the same country shepherds living out in the fields, keeping watch over their flock by night. And behold, an angel of the Lord stood before them, and the glory of the Lord shone around them, and they were greatly afraid. Then the angel said to them, "Do not be afraid, for behold, I bring you good tidings of great joy which will be to all people. For there is born to you this day in the city of David a Saviour, who is Christ the Lord."
>
> LUKE 2: 8–11

Fig 22

The kneeling figure – use for the kneeling shepherd and the Wise Man, Melchior.

Fold into this position (below) and glue or staple in place. Angle to lean slightly as shown, and bend the head slightly too. The kneeling figure can lean either forwards or back. The knitted figures are shown with the shepherd leaning back (holding the lamb) and the Wise Man, Melchior, leaning forwards to offer his gift.

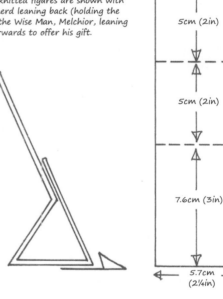

10cm (4in)

5cm (2in)

5cm (2in)

7.6cm (3in)

5.7cm (2¼in)

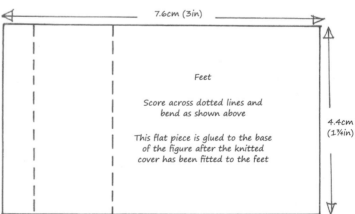

7.6cm (3in)

4.4cm (1¾in)

Feet

Score across dotted lines and bend as shown above

This flat piece is glued to the base of the figure after the knitted cover has been fitted to the feet

The short waistcoat (vest) is made in a neutral shade of D.K. yarn on size 3.75mm (UK 9, US 5)needles. Leave longish ends and cast on 14 sts. Knit 2 rows.

Row 3: p.11, k.3.
Row 4: k.
Repeat these 2 rows once more.
Row 7: (W.S. facing) cast off 10 sts. and k. to end of row.
Rows 8, 9, 10 and 11: k. 4 sts.
Row 12: k. 4, turn and cast on 10 sts.
Row 13: k. 14.
Row 14: k.
Row 15: p. 11, k. 3.
Repeat rows 14 and 15 ten more times.
Next row: k.3, p.11.
Next row: cast off 10 sts. (k.wise) and k. to end of row.
Next row: k.4 sts.
Next row: k.4 sts.
Next row: k.4, turn and cast on 10 sts.
Next row: p.11, k.3.
Next row: k.14.

Repeat the last 2 rows once more. Knit 2 complete rows and cast off k. wise. Sew the shoulders tog. then slip the garment on to the figure.

The lamb does not stand up like the others but just tucks underneath the shepherd's arm. From card, cut one body shape and one head shape, (see Fig 23), and make a rectangle of knitting to cover the body on both sides, folded over the back ridge. You will need about 20 sts. on size 3.75mm (UK 9, US 5) needles and about 22 rows, using any small amounts of lamb-coloured D.K. yarn.

For the head, make a small knitted rectangle to the size of the dotted lines on the diagram, and complete the making-up in the same way as for the other sheep. Tuck the lamb under the shepherd's arm as shown and glue it in position. Join the shepherd's hands together underneath with a stitch.

Fig 23

Knitting

Head – cut one in card

3.2cm (1¼in)

19mm (¾in)

Lamb

Body – cut one in card

13mm (½in)

6.4cm (2½in)

Standing shepherd with jerkin and white head-dress

As very little of the face shows on this model, (see Fig 24), no hair is needed, only embroidered eyes and a brown beard.

Make the face in the same way as Joseph's (see page 22). For the beard, use brown eyelash yarn and size 3mm (UK 11, US 3) needles. Cast on 10 sts. and work 7 rows in single rib, then cast off. Sew this piece on to the lower half of the face, pulling the top edge to reach the sides and sewing it into a curve.

The full length gown is made in a thickish multicoloured D.K. yarn, and only a small amount is needed – less than 20g. Use size 4mm (UK 8, US 6) needles and cast on 48 sts., working the first 8 rows in s.s.

Next row: (k2tog., k.4) 8 times, (40 sts.).

Continue in s.s. for 42 rows measured from the cast-on edge, or 15cm (6in), then work 2 rows of picot pattern at the neck, (see page 8). Cast off. Sew up the back seam and make a cord long enough to go through the neck holes. Slip the gown on to the figure, draw up the cord and tie. Glue the lower edge of the gown to the card base.

The sleeves are made separately from the hands. Using the same yarn and needles, cast on 4 sts. and work in s.s. for 2 rows. Now inc. 1 st. at each end of every k. row until there are 16 sts. Work 4 more rows in s.s., then change to g.st. for 4 rows. Cast off. Make another in the same way.

Using the same yarn as for the face, make the hands as folls.: with size 3mm (UK 11, US 3)needles, cast on 8 sts. and work 8 rows in s.s. Gather the last row on to a thread and sew up the side seam. Turn to the right side and insert the hands into the sleeve openings. Sew together. Attach the sleeve/hands to the body in the same way as previous models.

The jerkin is made in a handspun wool of roughly D.K. thickness. Your measurements can be checked against your card figure. Use size 3.75mm (UK 9, US 5) needles and note that the reverse side of s.s. is the R.S. Cast on 20 sts. and work from one front edge to the other. Work 8 rows in rev.s.s., then cast off 14 sts. and k. to the end of the row. Work 3 more rows, then turn and cast on 14 sts. Work 8 more rows on these 20 sts., then shape the back neck by casting off 4 sts. at the beg. of the next row, then p. to the end. Work 13 more rows ending with a k. row. Cast on 4 sts. to complete the neck and work 8 rows.

Cast off 14 sts. at the beg. of the next row and p. to the end. Work 3 rows on the rem. 6 sts., then cast on 14 sts. Work 8 rows on these 20 sts. and then cast off.

If the piece tends to curl badly, soak it in warm water, squeeze gently, then pin it out to dry naturally, blocking it into shape. Sew up the shoulder seams and slip the garment on to the figure as shown.

The white head-dress is made from a white D.K. yarn in the shape of a large triangle, but is not as large as Mary's head-dress. The front, (cast-on), edge should measure at least 18cm (7 in) wide, so use size 4mm (UK 8, US 6) needles and cast on 40 sts. Knit the first two rows and p. the 3rd row.

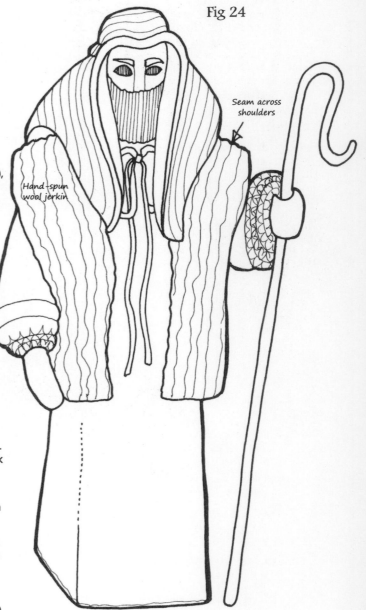

Fig 24

Seam across shoulders

Hand-spun wool jerkin

Now dec. 1 st. at each end of the next and every alt. k. row until only 2 sts. rem. Cast off.

Place the cast-on edge at the front of the head and pull well forward. To keep the head-dress in place, you can pin the two side points on to the front of the jerkin and sew them in place, and do the same with the back point. Make a thick cord to go round the head as shown, and stitch this securely in place to help hold the white cloth on.

The crook is made from a length of sturdy bendable wire about 25cm (10in) long. If the wire you have is too fine, bend it double, or make a 4-thickness piece to this length. Fold a piece of double-sided sticky-tape over the two ends and wrap the whole length with pale brown yarn until the wire is completely covered. The last end can be darned in. Using pliers, bend the end into a crook shape as shown then sew the shepherd's hand around the staff.

Finish by embroidering the features on to the face.

43

Standing shepherd with striped head-dress

Make the face and beard in the same way as Joseph's (see page 22), using eyelash yarn for the beard.

The pale blue undergown is simply a narrow panel glued to the front of the card base in the same way as Joseph's, so follow the same instructions as those on page 22 and glue it in position.

A multicoloured, random-dyed D.K. yarn was used for the overgown. You will need about 20g of this. Use size 4mm (UK 8, US 6) needles and cast on 40 sts. Knit 3 rows.

4th row: k.4, p. to the last 4 sts., k.4.
5th row: k.

Repeat these two rows until the piece measures 18cm (7in) from the beg. Now work the 2 rows of picot pattern, (see page 8). Cast off. Make a matching cord to go through the holes.

For the sleeves, use size 3.75mm (UK 9, US 5) needles and cast on 16 sts. Knit 2 rows. Beginning with a p. row, work 13 rows of s.s.

Next row: (k2tog.) 8 times.
Next row: p.

Cast off and sew up the side edges.

For the blue undersleeves and hands, use the blue yarn and size 3.75mm (UK 9, US 5) needles and cast on 10 sts. Work 7 rows in s.s. and knit the 8th row. Change to size 3mm (UK 11, US 3) needles and the same yarn as for the face and work 4 rows in s.s. Gather the last row on to a length of yarn to form the end of the hand. Sew up the side seams and insert the blue sleeve/hand into the outer sleeve opening. Glue or sew this in place.

G. st. border

Fig 25

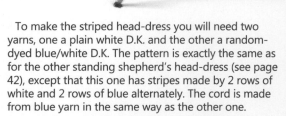

To make the striped head-dress you will need two yarns, one a plain white D.K. and the other a random-dyed blue/white D.K. The pattern is exactly the same as for the other standing shepherd's head-dress (see page 42), except that this one has stripes made by 2 rows of white and 2 rows of blue alternately. The cord is made from blue yarn in the same way as the other one.

Attach the multicoloured gown to the body, draw up the cord and tie. Glue the lower edges of the gown to the base, slightly overlapping the blue gown. Sew the two sleeves/hands in position angled slightly towards the front. Embroider the features, and arrange the head-dress on to the head, then sew firmly with the cord over this as shown. The crook is made in the same way as the other standing shepherd's, and can then be fixed into one of the hands.

44

...the shepherds said to one another,
"Let us now go to Bethlehem and
see this thing that has come to
pass..." And they came with haste
and found Mary and Joseph, and
the Babe lying in a manger.
LUKE 2: 15–16

Angel

For the face, use a pale, skin-coloured yarn and follow the instructions as for Mary, (see page 16). Use glitter yarns for the hair to the same thickness as D.K.: two metallic yarns used together made our model's hair, one gold and the other white pearl. Use size 3.75mm (UK 9, US 5) needles and cast on 12 sts. Work in rev. s.s. for about 23 rows then cast off. Gather up along one long edge, make this fit the top of the head and finish off with a few long stitches over the forehead. Embroider the features on to the face.

The gown is a simple rectangle with no shaping and holes at the neckline allow a cord to be passed through. As you will use whatever suitable yarns you have for this, measurements have been given as well as numbers of stitches and rows, so check with these at all stages. For our model, a white D.K. shiny yarn was used, (a 25g ball should be enough for both gown and wings), and size 3.75mm (UK 9, US 5) needles.

Cast on 50 sts. and begin at the base; this should measure at least 20cm (8in) wide. Continue in s.s. (with the addition of a few rev. s.s. rows here and there at the beginning), until the piece measures 15.5cm (6in) long. Now work two rows of picot pattern to make holes for the cord (see page 8). Knit 2 more rows and then cast off.

Sew up the back seam, and make a cord for the neck. Draw this up and tie in position on the figure. Glue the lower edge to the card base.

For the sleeves, use the same yarn and needles and cast on 16 sts. Knit 3 rows, then change to gold and k. 2 rows. Now knit one more row of white.

Next row: p.

Continue in s.s. for 12 more rows, then on the next row, (k2tog., k.5) twice, k2tog.

Next row: p.
Next row: (k2tog.) 6 times, k.1.
Next row: p.
Next row: k2tog., cast off 3 sts., k2tog., and cast off rem. st.

Sew up the side seams as far as the shaping and leave the rest open.

For the hands, use size 2.75mm (UK 12, US 2) needles and the same flesh-coloured yarn as for the face. Cast on 8 sts. and work 8 rows in s.s. Gather all the sts. on to a thread and draw up to form the end of the hand. Sew the side seams, insert the hands into the ends of the sleeves and sew, or glue, in place. Pin the sleeves/hands in position on the body, with the top of the sleeves on the same level as the neck gathering. Open out the top edges of the sleeves and angle the arms slightly forwards. Sew in position.

For the wings, (see Fig 26) make a base of firm white card. If your angel is to be seen from both back and front, you will need to make two sets of wings and stick these back to back on the card.

With size 6mm (UK 4, US 10) needles, and any shiny white D.K. yarn, cast on 96 sts.

Row 1: * k.5, p.2, rep. from * to last 5 sts., k. 5.
Row 2: * p.5, k. 2, rep. from * to last 5 sts., p.5.

Work 8 rows in this pattern.

Next row: * k2tog., k.1, k2tog., p.2, rep. from * to last 5 sts., k2tog., k.1, k2tog. (68 sts.).
Next row: * p.3, k.2, rep. from * to last 3 sts., p.3.
Next row: using a sparkling yarn of the same thickness (we used doubled metallic, one gold and one pearly) * k.3, p.2, rep. from * to the last 3 sts., k.3.

Change back to white yarn. Now work in pattern for 7 rows, then dec. again as folls:

Next row: * k3tog., p.2, rep. from * to last 3 sts., k3tog.
Next row: * p.1, k.2, rep. from * to last st., p.1.

Change to size 4mm (UK 8, US 6) needles and work 2 more rows in pattern.

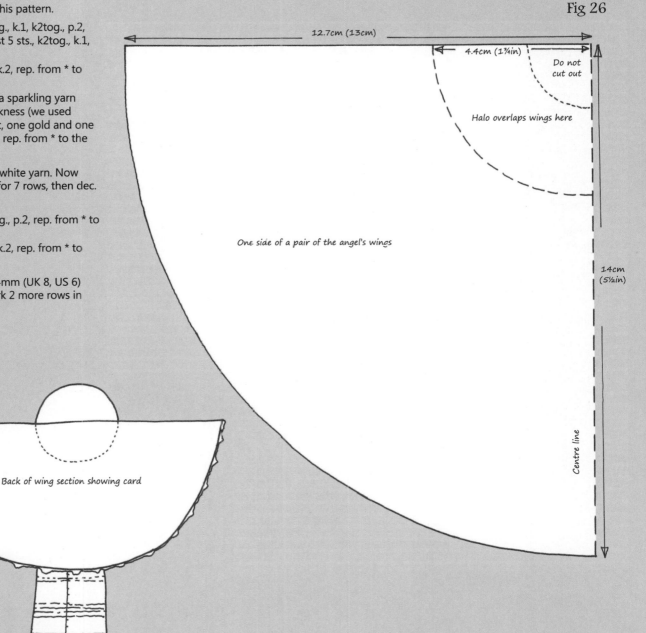

Fig 26

12.7cm (13cm)

4.4cm (1¾in)

Do not cut out

Halo overlaps wings here

One side of a pair of the angel's wings

14cm (5½in)

Centre line

Fig 27

Back of wing section showing card

47

Next row: k.1 * p2tog., k.1, rep. from * to last st., k.1.
Next row: work in single rib across all sts., then gather the rem. sts. on to a length of yarn and draw up. Darn all ends in.

Gather the top edge to fit the small area left uncovered on the card and glue the wings along the top edges first, allowing the edges of the knitting to project a little beyond the card. Now glue the curved edge and ease the knitting into position (see Fig 27, page 47).

To make the halo, follow the instructions for an adult halo on page 21. Glue the complete halo on to the top edge of the wings as shown, (see Fig 28), to overlap the knitting by about 2.5cm (1in).

The angel should now be glued into position on the wings so that the head is in the centre of the halo. Glue the arms angled outwards, or folded across the front of the body if preferred.

Fig 28

Halo stuck to wing section

Gold line

Glue hands in this position

And suddenly there was with the angel a multitude of the heavenly host praising God and saying: "Glory to God in the highest, and on earth peace, goodwill toward men!"

LUKE 2:13–14

Wise Men

Caspar: the Egyptian wise man in yellow and gold

The face-covering is dark brown and the features are embroidered. Make the face as for Mary, (see page 16). Hair is not necessary as the huge turban covers the head.

To make the turban, use a bright, multicoloured D.K. yarn together with a gold metallic yarn on size 3.75mm (UK 9, US 5) needles. Using the multicoloured yarn, cast on 18 sts. and work in s.s. for 54 rows, then cast off.

Sew the cast-on and the cast-off edges together and run a gathering thread around the outer edges of the tube. Draw up one edge to form the top, pad inside to fill out the shape, and draw up the lower edge to fit closely round the head. Do not stitch to the head yet, but secure the thread. Now make a very long crochet chain using the metallic glitter yarn only and thread this through a heavy needle. Wind it round and round the turban, using the needle to insert it through the top and out again through the bottom, pulling gently to fix the padding in position. Arrange the chain to lie in bands about 2.5cm (1in) apart, then secure it inside.

The pointed dome on top of the turban is made on the same needles in metallic yarn. Cast on 18 sts. and work in s.s. for 8 rows. On the next row, k2tog. across all sts. then gather these on to a length of yarn and draw up. Sew this shape into a dome, padding the inside very lightly and sew it to the centre of the turban as shown. Do not glue the turban to the head until the clothes have been fitted.

For the yellow gown, you will need about 20g of bright yellow D.K. yarn and size 3.75mm (UK 9, US 5) needles, several small balls of darker and paler yellow yarns, and metallic and multicoloured contrasts.

Cast on 50 sts. and k. 2 rows. Work 4 rows in double moss st. then change to the multicoloured yarn and work 4 more rows of double moss st. Add the metallic yarn and use it together with the dark yellow, k. one row and p. the next. Cut the metallic yarn and leave the dark yellow hanging free. Change to pale yellow, p. one row and k. the next. Repeat these 2 rows.

Break off the pale yellow and pick up the dark yellow, k. one row and p. one row.

Next row (dec. row): (k.3, k2tog.) 10 times, (40 sts.).

Break off dark yellow. Change back to pale yellow and p. one row. Now continue in double moss st. until the piece measures 14cm (5½in) from the beginning when slightly stretched. Now change to s.s. for 12 more rows, then work 2 rows of picot pattern, (see page 8). Cast off.

Darn in all loose ends on to the W.S. and fold across with the R.S.s tog. Sew up the side edges, taking care to match the coloured bands and using the same colours to sew them. Make a cord for the neckline and thread this through the holes. Slip the gown on to the figure and tie the cord.

To make the two sleeves, begin with the dark yellow yarn and cast on 30 sts. K. the first 2 rows and p. the third. Bring in the multicoloured yarn, k. the 4th row.

Row 5: k., then cut off this yarn.
Row 6: in dark yellow, k.
Row 7: bring in the gold (metallic) yarn and knit this together with the dark yellow.
Row 8: with the same 2 yarns, p.
  Cut both these yarns off and bring in the pale yellow.

Row 9: p.
Rows 10 to 13: double moss st.
Row 14: work in s.s., dec. as folls: (k2tog., k.3) 6 times.
Row 15: p.24.
Row 16: (k2tog., k.6) 3 times.
Row 17: p.
Row 18: k2tog. at beg. and end of the row.
Rows 19 and 20: as rows 17 and 18.
Row 21: p2tog. across all sts. to the last st., p.1.

Cast off. Darn all ends in and sew the two side edges together, matching stitches and colours.

  For the arms and hands, use dark brown yarn as for the face, and size 3.25mm (UK 10, US 3) needles. Cast on 12 sts. and work 14 rows in s.s. Leave the yarn hanging free, and bring in the gold (metallic) yarn.

Rows 15 and 16: k.
Row 17: p.
Row 18: k., do not cut the gold.
Row 19: with dark brown, k.
Row 20: p.
Row 21: with gold, k.
Row 22: k., cut off the gold yarn.

Continue in s.s. in dark brown for 6 more rows.

Next row: (k2tog.) 6 times.

  Draw these 6 sts. on to a thread and gather them up to form the end of the hand. With R.S.s tog., sew up the side edges, turn to the R.S. and pad very lightly. Insert the open end of the arm well into the sleeve matching the two sets of seams, and pin in place. Run a gathering thread all round the cast-on edge of the sleeve and draw this up to fit the arm closely just above the first gold bracelet. Sew the arm and sleeve together.

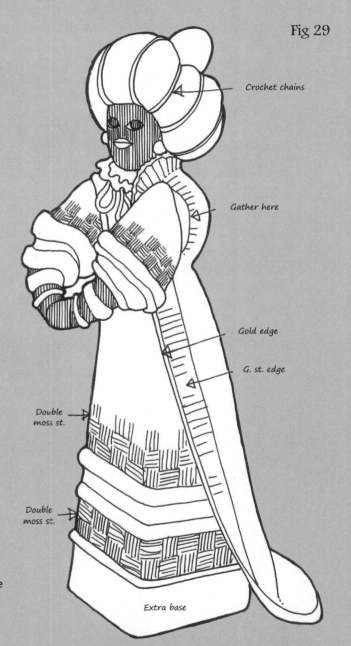

Fig 29

Crochet chains

Gather here

Gold edge

G. st. edge

Double moss st.

Double moss st.

Extra base

Pin the top of the sleeve to the body just below the neck cord, and angle it slightly towards the front with the seams to the inside. Sew both sleeves in place. Glue the bottom edge of the gown to the card.

The sleeveless coat and train have been knitted in deep gold D.K. yarn on size 4mm (UK 8, US 6) needles. An edge of gold (metallic) yarn has been crocheted around this garment, but could be embroidered if you prefer.

Cast on 20 sts. and knit the first row.

Row 2: inc., k. to last st., inc.
Row 3: k.4, p. to last 4 sts., k.4.

Repeat these last 2 rows until there are 30 sts. Keep straight in this pattern, knitting the first and last 4 sts. of every p. row, until the piece measures 18cm (7in) from the cast-on edge, ending with a p. row.

Divide for the arm-holes as folls:
Next row: k.5, cast off 3, k.14 (including the one on the needle), cast off 3, k.5 (including the one on the needle).

Work on the first set of 5 sts. in g.st. for 15 rows.

Cast off. Rejoin the yarn to the centre 14 sts.

Row 1: k.4, p.6, k.4.
Row 2: k.

Repeat these 2 rows 6 more times, then the first row once more. Cast off. Rejoin the yarn to the last 5 sts. and complete as for the other side.

Pin the piece out flat and press gently under a damp cloth. Sew up the shoulder seams and darn all ends in on the W.S. To make the arm-holes fit more closely at the back, fit the coat on to the figure, then run a gathering thread through the fabric where it bulges, and draw up to fit. Fasten off securely. Sew large beads to each side of the head to represent ear-rings, then glue the turban well down on to the head. Stitch the ends of the two hands together as shown so that they will support the casket of frankincense.

Now after Jesus was born in Bethlehem of Judea in the days of Herod the king, behold, wise men from the East came to Jerusalem, saying, "Where is He who has been born King of the Jews? For we have seen His star in the East and have come to worship Him."

MATTHEW 2:1–2

Balthazar: Persian wise man in green and red

A dark flesh colour is used for the face, which is made in the same way as for the other wise men, (see Fig 30 opposite). He has a very dark beard, and his hair is not worked on the top of his head as this is covered by his tall head-dress. Use a dark brown yarn.

Using size 3.75mm (UK 9, US 5) needles, cast on 19 sts. for the hair and work in single rib for 6 rows, i.e. 2cm (¾in).

Next row: rib 7, cast off 5 centre sts., rib 7.

Working on each side separately, rib 5, k2tog.

Next row: p2tog., rib 4.
Next row: rib 3, k2tog.
Next row: p2tog., rib 2.

Cast on 5 sts. then rib across all 8 sts. Work one more row across these sts. then cast off in rib. Break the yarn and rejoin it to the other 7 sts.

Next row: k2tog., rib 5.
Next row: rib 4, p2tog.
Next row: k2tog., rib 3.
Next row: rib 2, p2tog.

Work 2 rows on these 3 sts. then cast off. Sew all short ends in, then sew together the two short edges on the forehead. Sew the hair to the head around the face and the back of the head, but leave the top uncovered for the moment.

For the beard, cast on 7 sts. and work 8 rows in single rib. Cast off. Sew this in position, attaching it to the hair at each side and allowing it to hang well down on to the chest. Embroider the eyes with dark yarn.

For the gold hat, make a card base from a tube measuring 4cm (1½in) diameter and 3cm (1¼in) deep. With size 3mm (UK 11, US 3) needles and gold (metallic) yarn, cast on 39 sts. Knit one row then change to green metallic yarn. Work rows 3 to 8 of the gown pattern (see below and opposite), then continue in gold and work in s.s. (beginning with a k. row) for 6 more rows.

14th row: p.

Cast off k.wise. Sew up the side edges and glue this to the tube. To make the top, cast on 38 sts. and work 3 rows in s.s. On the next row, p2tog. across all sts. (19 sts.). Thread these sts. on to a length of yarn and draw up tightly, using the same yarn to sew the 2 short edges together. Even out the gathers to make a circle and sew the outer edge to the top edge of the hat. A large green sequin has been sewn to the centre of the hat. This can now be fitted to the head of the figure and glued into position.

Fig 30

The pattern used on the gown and the sleeves, needs 2 colours shown here as red and green.

Rows 1 and 2: with red yarn, k. Do not break yarn.
Row 3: with green yarn, (k.3, sl.1) to the last 3 sts., k.3.
Row 4: green, (p.3, sl.1) to the last 3 sts, p.3.
Rows 5 and 6: repeat rows 3 and 4.
Rows 7 and 8: red, repeat rows 1 and 2.
Row 9: green, k.1, (sl.1, k.3) to last 2 sts., sl.1, k.1.
Row 10: green, p.1, (sl.1, p.3) to last 2 sts., sl.1, p.1.
Rows 11 and 12: repeat rows 9 and 10.

These 12 rows form the pattern.

The green and red robe is knitted in a very simple slip-stitch pattern, (see above), and requires about 20g of green and a small amount of red in the same thickness D.K. Use size 3.75mm (UK 9, US 5) needles and cast on 47 sts. Knit 3 rows. Now work 5 complete patterns, (i.e. 60 rows), then repeat rows 1 to 8 again. Break off the green yarn and work the 2 rows of picot pattern in red (see page 8). Cast off. Sew up the 2 side edges, make a cord and thread this through the neck holes.

To make the sleeves, cast on 22 sts. with red yarn and k. 3 rows. Do not break off red, but change to green and work rows 3 to 8 of pattern. Break off red yarn and k. one row of green, then p. one row. Continue to work in s.s., and dec. one st. at end of next and every foll. k. row until there are 8 sts. left. Purl one more row and then cast off.

To make the under-sleeves and hands, with the metallic green yarn and size 3mm (UK 11, US 3) needles, cast on 14 sts. Work 7 rows in s.s., beginning with a k. row. Knit the 8th row and break off the green yarn, changing to the face-coloured yarn to work 4 rows in s.s.

Next row: (k2tog.) 7 times, (7 sts.).

Gather the last sts. on to a thread and draw up to form the end of the hand. Make another in the same way. Sew up the side seams, pad very lightly and glue this piece into the sleeve opening. Sew the sleeves on to the shoulder area of the body, just below the neckline.

Sequin

Extra base

55

For the cloak, a red mottled D.K. yarn was used, but any other appropriate yarn will do as well. You will need about 20g and size 4mm (UK 8, US 6) needles. Cast on 30 sts. and k. 3 rows. Continue in s.s., but to prevent the sides from rolling inwards, make a border of g.st. at the beginning and end of every row. Work 60 rows.

Next row (dec. row): (k2tog.) 15 times.

Work in the single rib for 10 rows for the collar. Cast off in rib. Darn the ends in, then gather across the base of the collar and sew this part to the shoulders, allowing the collar to fall back. Glue the edge of the gown to the card base all round the lower edge, and join the hands together with a stitch as shown in the photograph so that they will support the casket of myrrh.

Melchior: Kneeling wise man in purple and silver

Fig 31

This wise man wears a purple gown with long sleeves gathered round the middle with cords, (see opposite). Over this he wears a richly-textured cloak. His white hair and long beard show him to be a senior member of the trio. The face is made in a light flesh-coloured yarn in the same way as the others, and the eyes are embroidered. He has white eyebrows.

Make the hair using white D.K. yarn and size 3.75mm (UK 9, US 5) needles. Cast on 19 sts. and work in moss st. for 18 rows.

Next row: (k2tog.) 9 times, k.1.

Gather these sts. on to a thread and draw up to form the top of the head. Fit this piece in position on top of the head, pulling the two lower corners well on to the face, and pin. Make the beard as folls:
cast on 2 sts. and knit them.

Row 2: inc. into both sts. to make 4.
Row 3: (k.1, p.1) twice.
Row 4: inc. into the first and last sts., keeping the single rib pattern correct.
Row 5: single rib on 6 sts.
Row 6: as row 4.

Work on these 8 sts. for 7 more rows, then cast off in rib and pin the beard in position. Sew the side edges of the beard to the hair, and the top edge to the face. Now sew the rest of the hair in place except round the lower edge which has to overlap the neck-opening.

The circlet of silver on the wise man's head is made from a ring of card measuring 4cm (1½in) diameter and 2cm (¾in) deep. This is covered, on the outside, with a strip of double-sided sticky-tape, and then wrapped with silver metallic yarn. The ends can be stuck down on to the inside with sticky-tape. The circlet is then glued well down on to the hair.

The purple gown requires about 20g of purple D.K. yarn and size 3.75mm (UK 9, US 5) needles. The measurements are basically the same as those needed for the kneeling shepherd's tunic, (which is made from a thicker yarn), so either set of instructions will do, (see page 38).

Cast on 52 sts. and work in double rib for 14 rows. This will measure roughly 22cm (8¾in) when stretched.

Row 15: (k2tog., p.2) 13 times.
Row 16: * k.2, p.1, rep. from * to end of row.
Row 17: * k.1, p.2, rep. from * to end of row.

Continue to repeat the last 2 rows until the piece measures 7.6cm (3in) from the beginning.

Now change to s.s. and continue until the piece measures 13cm (5in) from the cast-on edge. Work 2 rows of picot st. to make a set of holes for the neck cord, (see page 8), then cast off. Make a 41cm (16in) cord for the neck, fold the knitted piece R.S.s together and sew up the two side edges. Turn to the R.S. and slip this over the card figure. Thread the cord through the neck holes and tie, then tuck the top edge of the gown under the hair and beard and sew in place.

To make the sleeves and hands, with the purple yarn, cast on 4 sts. and work 2 rows in s.s. Now inc. one st. at each end of next and every foll. knit row until there are 16 sts. On the next 2 rows, work the picot pattern to make a set of holes, (see page 8).

Next row: (k.1, inc. 1) 8 times, to make 24 sts. in all.
Now work 7 rows in single rib.
Next row: (k2tog.) 12 times to make 12 sts.

Change to size 3mm (UK 11, US 3) needles and k. one row. Break off the purple yarn and change to face colour. Work 8 rows in s.s. in this colour, then, on the 9th row, p2tog. across all sts. Draw the last sts. on to a length of yarn and gather to form the end of the hand. With the R.S.s tog., sew the hand up, then use purple yarn to sew the sleeve seam from the hand end to just past the picot holes. Leave the rest open. Turn to the R.S. and pad the lower part of the sleeve very lightly but not the hand. Pin the sleeve in position on the shoulder and make another one in the same way. Sew the sleeves to the body, slightly angled forwards, around the openings at the tops of the sleeves.

Make the feet in the same way as for the kneeling shepherd and fix them in position on the body (see page 38). Pad the top of the knees between the card and the gown, and then glue the lower edge of the gown to the card base.

The cloak fastens round the neck by two projections, and the yarn used should be the most sumptuous D.K. you can find. As the knitting is seen from the reverse side (rev.s.s.), the yarn should preferably be a slub one with a bumpy texture for the most impact. Basically, it is made as follows: use size 3.75mm (UK 9, US 5) needles and cast on 40 sts. Work 6 rows in rev.s.s.

Cast off 10 sts. and work 16 more rows on the rem 30 sts. Now cast on 10 sts., (at the same edge), for the other shoulder projection and work 6 rows on these 40 sts., then cast off. Sew the 2 short edges together to form a hole for the head, slip the head through this and arrange the cloak to hang behind. Darn all ends in. On the illustrated version, two different yarns have been used, one for a border and one for the centre portion. A narrow border of crochet has been worked in silver thread round the edge, to help to keep it flat. The piece may need to be pressed lightly under a damp cloth.

Make short cords for the sleeve decoration and thread these through the holes to tie in bows.

And when they had come into the house, they saw the young Child with Mary His mother, and fell down and worshiped Him. And when they had opened their treasures, they presented gifts to Him: gold, frankincense, and myrrh.

MATTHEW 2: 11

59

Gold, frankincense and myrrh

Three caskets may be placed in the arms of the three wise men or laid on the stable floor at the feet of Mary, though the kneeling wise man has placed his there already, (see page 62). For these small caskets, (see Fig 32), pieces of card and tubes will be required, and the knitted covers can be embellished with beads and sequins. The amounts of yarn needed are extremely small, but metallic ones are particularly useful, as are fine yarns, such as shiny embroidery threads, which can be used double.

Fig 32

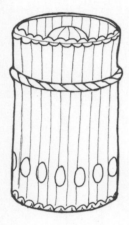
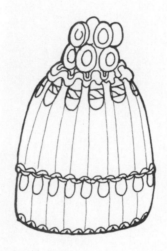

Gold

Make the card base (see Fig 33). Cover this with a piece of knitting using a metallic gold yarn and size 3mm (UK 11, US 3) needles. For this, you should cast on 30 sts. and work 4 rows of s.s., 2 rows of rev.s.s., 12 rows of s.s., 2 rows of picot pattern (see page 8), 2 rows of s.s., 2 rows of rev.s.s., then p2tog. across all sts. to make 15. K. one more row, draw sts. on to a thread and gather up to form the base.

Stitch up the two sides to form a tube and fit this on to the card tube. Sew and glue this in position and place jewels, beads or sequins in the centre. Our version has a chain (crocheted) of the same yarn tied at the top, with some gold sequins for extra decoration.

Frankincense

Make the card tube (see Fig 33). Use a taupe yarn, or similar, to make a strip of knitting on size 3mm (UK 11, US 3) needles. Cast on 40 sts. and work 4 rows in s.s., 3 in rev.s.s., then 3 more rows in s.s. Now work 2 rows of picot pattern, (see page 8), but k. the 2nd row instead of p., then work 6 more rows in s.s. and 2 more rows of picot pattern. Now work 2 rows of rev.s.s., and on the last p2tog. across all sts. to make 20. Finish with one more k. row and then cast off. Sew up in the same way as the gold casket, and make a cord or chain to go through the holes for decoration. Add beads to the top (see Fig 32).

Myrrh

You will need a piece of firm card measuring 7.6 x 10cm (3 x 4in). Divide this up as shown (see Fig 34 opposite) to form the cube which is the base around which to fit the knitted piece. Your piece of knitting will be exactly the same shape and size as this piece of card. Use silver metallic yarn and size 3mm (UK 11, US 3) needles, and cast on 9 sts. Now follow the graphic instructions on Fig 34. Sew up the sides in the same way as you assembled the cube, sewing from the W.S. and slipping the card cube inside before you sew up the last seams.

A plastic curtain ring was wrapped with the same yarn and glued to the top for decoration, and jewels and sequins can be added as you wish, but the effect is more delicate if you try to keep them small in proportion to the box, (see Fig 32).

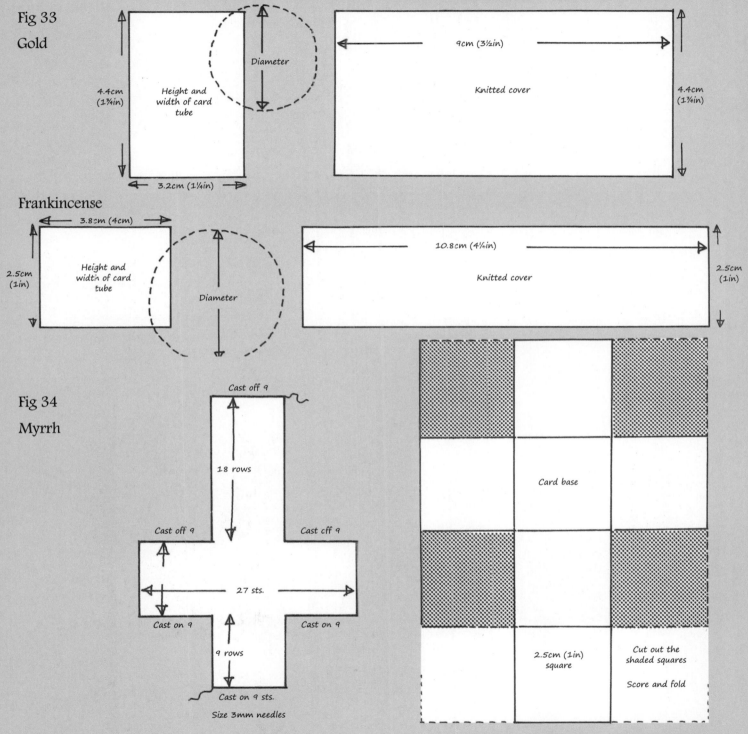

Fig 33
Gold

4.4cm (1¾in) — Height and width of card tube — Diameter

3.2cm (1¼in)

9cm (3½in) — Knitted cover — 4.4cm (1¾in)

Frankincense

3.8cm (4cm)

2.5cm (1in) — Height and width of card tube — Diameter

10.8cm (4¼in) — Knitted cover — 2.5cm (1in)

Fig 34
Myrrh

Cast off 9

18 rows

Cast off 9   Cast off 9

27 sts.

Cast on 9   Cast on 9

9 rows

Cast on 9 sts.

Size 3mm needles

Card base

2.5cm (1in) square

Cut out the shaded squares

Score and fold

61

Publishers' Note

If you would like more books about
novelty knitting and crochet, try:

Twenty to Make: Mini Christmas Knits
by Sue Stratford, Search Press 2011

Twenty to Make: Mini Christmas Crochet
by Val Pierce, Search Press 2011

If you would like more information on knitting
techniques, try:

Beginner's Guide to Knitting by
Alison Dupernex, Search Press 2004